Repentance

MG Bennett

Author: MG Bennett

Publisher: T. Nelson

London

The Biblical quotes are usually from NIV

"Give me one hundred preachers who despise nothing, but sin and desire nothing but God, and I care not whether they be clergymen or laymen, they alone (by Christ in them) will shake the gates of Hell and set up the kingdom of Heaven upon Earth."

John Wesley
(Paraphrased)

FOREWORD

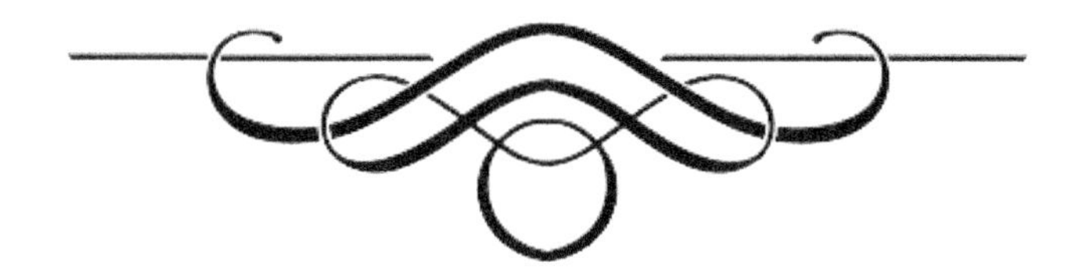

Having worked alongside MG Bennett for over 7 years I know he is a gifted teacher.

He loves debating, discussing, and encouraging. This book is him at his classic best, wanting to explain hard concepts gently but clearly.

You will go on a journey with him and you will be challenged and educated!

Revd. Canon Jeremy Fraser
(Missions and Evangelism Episcopal Advisor)

This is a magnificent book! The argument and structure are easy to follow. There are some passages which particularly impressed me, those about the Temple and about Paul & Damascus.

I also liked the realistic view of the Christian life, with its ups and downs, and the description of the way in which we become faithful disciples, over time, with discipline.

The Revd. Brian McHenry CBE

Table of Contents

EXPLANATION OF THE IMPORTANCE OF REPENTANCE

Many of us, almost instinctively, know (or think we know) what repentance is: it is to turn away from sin and toward God, to live the way God wants and to obey Him. This is indeed repentance in a brief outline, but there are some extremely useful and helpful features of it, which we will look at a bit later.

We will start first with explaining the importance of repentance before we delve into the details of its nature in the next chapter.

The very first call to action and may be the very first word Jesus said in preaching openly to the world was *"Repent":*

Matthew, also called Levy, one of Jesus' apostles, wrote "Repent for the Kingdom of God has come" (Matthew 3:2)

The Evangelist Mark similarly recorded Him saying

"The time has been fulfilled and the Kingdom of God has drawn near, repent and believe the Gospel"
(Mark 1:15)

Jesus is the King and with Him the Kingdom of God was approaching in an unparalleled way, but precisely because of this advance of God's kingdom the people were called to repent or turn to God.

It is like an army of holiness nearing a city and the inhabitants, who are not holy at all, exactly the opposite, are called to surrender and not only that, but also join the advancing army. It is a matter of life and death.

We should realise that God is absolutely just, holy, and perfect and He requires nothing less from each of us. Every bad thing we intended, have said, and done will be accounted for before the holy Governor and Judge. Yet, due to Him being loving and merciful, He does not want to mete out the consequences of our bad works on us, but He says, *"turn to Me"* or *"repent"*.

Let me take you to another city, called Jerusalem, about 2000 years ago, when Jesus lived in the lands of Israel. Something outstandingly horrible happened.

It was a warm day in the city and a special one at that: Yom Kippur, the day of atonement, when hundreds of thousands of Jewish worshippers swooped on the holy capital of once independent Israel and offered millions of animal sacrifices to God. The notion of sacrifice was the bedrock of their Holy Scriptures (the part of the Bible that we call "Old Testament" [OT]) and it comprised about one thirds of the Law of Moses (the man who traditionally was believed to have written the first five and foundational books of the OT in which the laws given from God to him are found). They were taught that sin: missing to do what God likes or doing what God detests is a profoundly serious matter because God is pure and holy. Sin therefore required sacrifice which symbolically showed how the consequences of the bad things committed by people are taken up by the innocent animals.

Sin, they knew, costs lives and therefore the life of a living being had to pay for it. Hence some animals were slaughtered and burnt, but others were symbolically laid hands on, and the sins of the people were confessed upon them and then they were left outside the city in a deserted place where they took and carried the sins with them away from the people. Another function of the sacrifices was for the people to thank God for His forgiveness and goodness by eating their meat and produce which they brought with them and by sharing it and giving it to the needy and poor and to the servants in God's Temple, the priests and Levites. It was a great day of repentance or turning to God, a day of social levelling and economic redistribution as all are equal before just God. The hearts of the people would think about their wrongs, they would confess this and turn from it and would sacrifice to God by burning the animals, which showed that He took away their sins from them. Everybody was happy and full of humility, gratitude, and food. Everybody would go back home, that was the intention of the holiday, satisfied that they have had their path straightened before their Creator.

There was a group of people from the home region of Jesus, Galilee, who did not come back home happy and content.

They did not come back at all. They indeed set out to worship God as prescribed in the Law, but something occurred which made the Roman governor Pilate think that they are bent to bring havoc and sedition. We have it on record (Josephus, an ancient Roman/Jewish historian of the 1st century) that Pilate killed numerous people for example for protesting his taxes over infrastructural projects or simply because they seemed bound to cause trouble by gathering in their multitudes to seek some holy items in the mountain called Gerizim. In one instance, Pilate likely thought that a gathering of Galilean pilgrims in Jerusalem might lead to rebellion and attacked the people and killed many of them. Public gatherings were strictly regulated in the Roman empire. These Galileans probably expressed some concerns or dissatisfaction with the authorities, which reached the ears of Pilate and his army fell on them whilst they were sacrificing. You can imagine, how the animals had just had their throats slashed by the priests, who were expert at this, and placed on the stone altar to be burnt, their blood still flowing and dripping down the rocks and in the canals around the altar, whilst the group of men were standing by, heads down, meditating or looking at what was happening when they were attacked, without any warning, by the Romans. It was a slaughter of people during the killing of animals and their blood was mixed up with each other. Some of the bystanders rushed out and alerted the city. The inhabitants and the numerous pilgrims would have done best to keep their mouths shut and heads down. It worked. Pilate asserted the Roman authority as it was meant to be.

The news reached Jesus, who was probably not far off from there with His disciples, when:

Some of those present at that time told Jesus about the Galileans whose blood Pilate had mixed with their sacrifices. Jesus answered,

"Do you think that these Galileans were worse sinners than all the other Galileans because they suffered this way? I tell you, no! But unless you repent, you too will all perish. Or those eighteen who died when the tower in Siloam fell on them—do you think they were more guilty than all the others living in Jerusalem? I tell you, no! But unless you repent, you too will all perish." (Luke 13:1-5).

Jesus did not make political comments and He did not focus on the tragedy of lost life although He said that the victims "suffered", which shows His compassion, but He used this occasion to hammer home a lesson, which would help other people avoid even a bigger tragedy for them. He first pointed out that they were not "bigger sinners" than the others, but implicitly He stated that they were sinners. Then He gave another example of a tragic death where hope and suffering were likewise mixed up. **The Pool of Siloam was a place of ritual and physical purification and Jesus sent a blind man (John 9:6-11)** there to wash his eyes and then he was able to see. It was not far, maybe about 100-150 yards from the Temple in Jerusalem. It had some large towers around it, some with a diameter of about 12 feet and a possible height of 40 feet. It was a place of rejuvenation, cleanliness, health, and life but it turned out to be deadly for 18 men who were nearby when the tower collapsed and fell over them. Notice how Jesus mentioned the exact number of the casualties, which again shows how important each single person was for Him. They were not just a group of men. They were 18 people with their hopes and dreams, thoughts, talk and actions. And yes, they were quite a large group to die so suddenly and together, so the accident was well remembered by most people around. Jesus then moves on to say the last thing that anybody would think of when hearing such news. He was not worried that some may accuse Him in using a tragedy to preach to those remaining. He, very straightforwardly, said:

"They perished and if you do not repent you will likewise perish too".

This cannot mean that all people will die in this way if they do not repent, because most people do not die in an accident. It could not mean that if the listeners do not repent, they will die. All people die one day, and this will be the case until Jesus comes. Rather Jesus warns everyone that if they do not repent, they will perish forever, for the whole of eternity. The salvation of the soul is directly related to the repentance of the heart and mind.

Repentance is the unavoidable milestone, the state of mind, which we all must reach and possess. John the Baptist preached repentance and baptism and he was upset and angry when people came for baptism and not for repentance. He would say

"Who warned you to run from the coming wrath (the consequences of their sins) you brood of vipers? Bear fruit worthy of repentance." (Matthew 3:8-10).

It has always been that the external ritual of baptism should reflect the internal spiritual reality of the heart and we are told to repent.

In Mark 6 and Matthew 10 Jesus is recorded sending out 70 people to preach the good news that His kingdom has come close to them. If they did not accept their message, those people, he warned:

"It will be more bearable to Sodom and Gomorrah on the day of judgement than for that town" (Matthew 10:15).

What did the 70 disciples of Jesus ask people to do in response to the advancing Kingdom of God?

In Mark 6:12 it says that

"They went down and preached that people should repent"!

That is the only adequate way in which one should respond to the Kingdom of God and the only way which spares one for its demand for justice and holiness.

The Apostle Paul was in court, instigated by the Jewish leaders, for allegedly causing nuisance and social uproar and disorder by preaching Jesus. He, in his defence, said that what he was preaching was the call to action which the Hebrew Scriptures (and later the New Testament). Paul said that he -

"Preached that they should repent and turn to God and demonstrate their repentance by their deeds." (Acts 26:20).

If you never or rarely hear sermons about the need to repent by turning to God and that repentance naturally flows into deeds which God likes and approves of, then you have missed to be exposed, as the early Christians were under the preaching of the apostles, to one of the most important messages in the Bible and a message which is foundational to your relationship with God and salvation.

James says in his epistle:

"Come close to God and He will come close to you" (James 4:8).

Repentance as a way of life ensures intimacy with God and answered prayers.

Your level of repentance determines your closeness with God.

It is the main ingredient (alongside complete trust in Jesus) of preaching the Gospel of Jesus Christ.

In Luke 24:47 Jesus says:

"repentance for the forgiveness of sins will be preached in My name to all nations, beginning at Jerusalem".

Gospel without call for repentance is void.

Jesus comes to give us repentance:

"God exalted him at his right hand as Leader and Saviour, to give repentance to Israel and forgiveness of sins" (Acts 5:31).

Have you received repentance from Him? If not or you are not sure then know that it is available to you. But we should ask another important question:

WHAT IS REPENTANCE?

In the Book of Deuteronomy, which is the fifth and last book traditionally believed to be written by the prophet Moses, God said that if the Israelites listen to God's voice they will be blessed and if they disregard His words they will be in trouble (or cursed). But if they disobeyed and the curse catches up with their evil works, they still had an opportunity to change their plight. They had to "return to God" and follow Him. This is the essence of repentance.

When all these blessings and curses I have set before you come on you and you take them to heart wherever Jehovah your God disperses you among the nations, and when you and your children return to the Lord your God and obey him with all your heart and with all your soul according to everything I command you today, then Jehovah your God will restore your fortunes and have compassion on you and gather you again from all the nations where he scattered you (Deut.30:1-3).

It will be helpful to our discourse to borrow the conceptual framework from the debate between the representatives of

Calvinism and Arminianism (movements in Christian theology in past centuries) regarding how salvation from the sins occurs and explain the process in more depth. The abbreviation TULIP (please bear with me, if this is a new material for you, it will become clear as you read along) stands for five Christian teachings on this topic, which are: Total depravity, Unconditional election, Limited atonement, Irresistible grace, and Perseverance of the saints. We will explore each of them in turn because they pertain to how repentance and salvation from the sins and eternal judgment happens.

TULIP

Total Depravity

Before we get to know Jesus, we are in a state of disobedience toward our Creator and we are slaves of sin and subjects of its consequences: curse and ultimately eternal death which is forever a separation from God.

The Bible clearly states that we all, in some way, have turned away from God.

"We all, like sheep, have gone astray,
each of us has turned to our own way;"
(Book of the prophet Isaiah 53:6).

Occasionally, people get tempted to think that they have nothing wrong on their record. We like to think about ourselves that we are "good" people. The standard of God though is perfection and holiness. Jesus said:

"Be perfect as your Heavenly Father is perfect
(Mathew 5:48).

This clearly shows that we all fail the standard of God. Isaiah was a prophet and he included himself in this. He said:

"we all ...have gone astray".

He realised his insufficiency to meet God's requirement of purity and holiness. King David, who traditionally wrote the Psalms and Apostle Paul in his epistles confirm that

"There is no one righteous, not even one" (Psalm 14:3; Romans 3:10).

We should accept that this is the case with humility because only then God can help us. He came to help those in need, not those who refuse help.

Why is then that the case? Why have all people sinned?

The apostle explains that:

"Therefore, just as sin entered the world through one man, and death through sin, and in this way, death came to all people, because all sinned " (Romans 5:12).

What is he talking about? He is referring to Adam and Eve in the early chapters of the Book of Genesis. Adam and Eve were created righteous and without sin. They had the free will to choose if they should listen to God's words or refuse to. They were told that they can eat anything they wish except for one tree in the Garden of Eden called **"The Tree of knowing good and evil".** There were thousands of options to do right and only one option to do wrong. Unfortunately, they were tricked by the devil (the chief evil spirit) who, through a creature, a serpent, told them that God lied to them and there would be no bad consequences if they sinned against God by mistrusting Him and eating from the tree. The result was that sin entered into humanity and with it entered death. Adam and Eve died toward God, they were no longer intimate with Him as He wished it to be and as it was before and so they had to be expelled from Eden. They did not die immediately, but after some time they did die. Sadly, sin and death passed from them into all people after them and this is so because we received from them the inclination to sin, a sinful nature, which the Bible calls "flesh" and we duly sinned too. It is important to point out that people do not inherit guilt from Adam and Eve, but they receive, when they are born, the tendency to like what is evil. It is unavoidable that everybody, even though born innocent and without sin, to commence sinning at some point. Children start to lie and be selfish from a young age for example. This is our nature, "the body of sin" as the Bible also calls it. In this state of being, we need education and training to manage the evil impulses and choices that come naturally to us and this every good parent is trying to do for their children. They know that all humans are prone to do evil and need to be taught otherwise. The problem is that no human being can teach another to be free from evil thoughts, words, or deeds altogether, because all of us are in the same spiritually broken boat. None of us is perfect. We should aim for what is good, but we should bear in mind that we need God to free us from this sinful, human nature which tends to do evil and sin to our own detriment. On our own we cannot change ourselves as God wants.

The only One who can help us and cancel our sins and change us, is God, whom we, tragically, do not know intimately and do not want to know about. The serious issue with this sinful nature is that we all, inside of us, have an attitude of rebellion against Him. That is how we are naturally. On our own we would not and we cannot come to Him. This is called total depravity. We are corrupted and the corruption is total. It is one thing to have flaws and seek remedy, but it is hugely different when we just do not want to seek God, against whom the sins are committed and who alone can help us. Of course, every one of us can be good in some ways even when we are without God. This, the theologians call, "the residual Image of God". We show something of our former glory, when God made us after His own image, but it is quite insufficient because we do not want to come to the One to whom we owe everything. Apostle Paul describes this as

"dead in our trespasses"
(Eph 2:1, Col 2:13).

Under this condition we are dead spiritually and without God as our God and Father, and a dead person cannot do much. We cannot and do not want to do anything to save ourselves by bringing ourselves closer to Him.

What does God do? He can see that we are foreign to Him and we would never return to Him if this depended on us alone. Yet, He can see, even before we were even born that there is hope, if He intervenes. There is nobody else who can salvage us from us, the dominance of sin and the lies of the devil in our lives, which we embrace, and God knows that unless He works inside of us as people and individuals, we will not come to Him and receive His life and His blessings.

Unconditional Election

What follows next? We saw that the state of total depravity toward God, its manifestation - sin, and its consequences -

suffering and death - is indisputable. All people sin, sin or bad actions have consequences to us and to other people, and all people are dead spiritually in this depraved state and are dying out physically too, which is a function of the spiritual death. All people who die without God in their lives, God being thus rejected, receive what they chose whilst alive - eternal separation from Him or hell.

We ask then: “Did God see this total human rebellion coming?” and the answer is “Yes”. God knew everything that would happen and what we will do. He knew about our future rebellion against Him. When you read this, if you have never come to Him yet, you may feel some disdain, and shake your head at this and be inclined to say, critically: “But why would God allow this?”. Many of us have felt this way and had an attitude of criticism about how things are at some point in time, being inclined to blame God for it, and this is another proof that we did not know Him and we were willing to believe things which paint Him and His words in the worst possible way. Placing guilt on God and not ourselves is the natural reaction of unregenerate humanity. “Unregenerate” means a person has not yet fully experienced God’s saving goodness and grace and has not lived through the conversion from this rebellious and adversarial mindset. It is not bad to ask such a question, but it is bad to assume an answer which puts the blame on God. That is typical of the rebel, but not the well-meaning, objective person. The good thing about this is that God saw this coming too. He knew about all the bad words people would say about Him. He knows that this is due to their depreciation and deprivation of Him. We do not know Him, when we are in an unregenerate state, but we also refuse to know Him for who He is. Knowing all this beforehand, God did not decline to make us anyway. He saw the problem clearly even before it existed and yet chose to create us. He chose to create every person, whether they will be relatively good one like the doctor who left his highly paid job to serve in Africa for next to no payment or relatively bad like a dictator who ordered the killing of millions. The question is "Why did God decide to create us anyway?"

There are three main reasons for this which have been revealed to us.

One reason is that God wanted to show how bad people who choose to be without Him could be. Not all people will pan out like Hitler, but all people, given the "right" circumstances can become monsters. The "right circumstances" are those in which the true, just, and loving God of the Bible is not present, which is to say not known and honoured, and there is a strong push, internal motivation, or external imposition, toward doing evil. Take for example the millions of "normal" people in Germany, who would commit atrocities and justify them with necessity. Evil is paradoxical and remains evil, even if sugar coated with "good" for the perpetrators, but in reality, who have fake motives. The only cure for evil is that people freely choose to tap into God's goodness, wisdom, power, justice, and holiness. Only then can we realise how bad we were and appreciate the change in us the God brought in. Therefore, showing us how bad we could become without Him and what it means to exist for the creation, if His laws are rejected, is one reason why He created us. These verses confirm this point:

So, I gave them over to their stubborn hearts to follow their own devices (Psalm 81:12).

Therefore, God gave them over in the sinful desires of their hearts (Romans 1:24a)

Jehovah has made everything for His purpose-- even the wicked for the day of evil (Proverbs 16:4)

This last verse shows that God knew that the evil people would choose to be evil (all of us) and remain (some of us) evil, but their existence has a purpose. It shows how bad "evil" is.

Another, twofold reason, which we derive from reading God's words, the Bible, is that God wanted to show His clear disapproval of sin and His ability, power, and glory to save people from it, with their own agreement, despite their weakness and corruption.

What if God, although choosing to show his wrath and make his power known, bore with great patience the objects of his wrath--prepared for destruction? What if he did this to make the riches of his glory known to the objects of his mercy, whom he prepared in advance for glory? (Romans 9:22,23).

We read here that God is angry at sin, the bad choices people made (it ruins them), but He is still patient with everybody: those who will choose to change and those who will persist in being evil and rejecting Him. He is patiently working with everyone to save us from our bad choices. He did not foresee the problem and decided to avoid it, but decided to tackle it head on, because He is able. If He were not able to save us from our sins, He would have never created us. This means that there would have never been beings with true and tested free wills. If we could not reject God, we are not totally free. If we could not be tested and had really made this choice to reject God, we may have always wondered if we were ever free at all. Now there is no doubt that we are made free.

This leads us to the third reason why God made us free to choose evil and reject Him despite knowing that we will choose to do that.

God is love (1 John 4:8).

God freely loves us because this is His nature and He wanted us to be the same like Him. We read that:

So, God created man in his own image; he created him in the image of God; he created them male and female (Gen 1:27).

He could have created beings which will never choose to abandon Him, practically unable to sin but it would not have been a real option for them and their relationship with Him would not have been the love that He requires and likes to see in us. He wants people who would love Him and be like Him even though they can choose and indeed can choose not to be so. This is true love. It is based on freedom. If there was no alternative, then we can question if it is free and real at all. God made us for Himself, "for His glory" as Scripture clearly says:

"everyone who is called by my name, whom I created for my glory, whom I formed and made." (Is 43:7)

But none is forced into this relationship. We are free to choose. We are free to love.

This seems contradictory to the first fact of human nature that we have discussed, that we are totally depraved, because this means that free will is gone and we are slaves of sin. God knew that we would choose to push Him aside and do our own thing regardless of Him, so was our free will lost for good? No. He also looked through the corridors of time and even though He saw that we will reject Him, all of us, He also saw that if He personally intervenes with each of us individually, in a special way, which we will discuss latter, many of us will stop our rebellion and choose to love Him. Without His radical work in us, we do not want Him, sadly, we have made our choice, but this choice is not our last word if we are exposed like a fruitless seed to His light and warmth like never previously in our lives.

The Bible reveals that:

"... those God foreknew he also predestined to be conformed to the image of his Son, that he might be the firstborn among many brothers and sisters. And those he predestined, he also called; those he called, he also justified; those he justified, he also glorified. (Romans 8:29,30)

Notice this:" those whom he foreknew". God looked before we even existed and saw what we will do. He made us in His image, so He made us all righteous:

This alone I found that God made human beings straightforward , but they have devised many schemes. (Eccl 7:29).

This shows that the seed of His Image is inside of each of us, but as we said already, we are in a position of slavery to sin and rebellion due to wrong choices. We would not and could not turn from this state of being. Can a slave in shackles free themselves? This is practically impossible. Can a dead person make themselves alive? This is impossible. But what is impossible for humankind is possible for God. God would not contradict and change His character, but He can change us. And before time began, He chose us for salvation. All people are called, but those who accept His call become eligible for salvation. Not every person agrees with God's offer to save and bless them forever:

For many are invited, but few are chosen." (Mathew 22:14).

"I called you so often, but you wouldn't come. I reached out to you, but you paid no attention (Proverbs 1:24).

But not all of them welcomed the good news. For Isaiah says, "Lord, who has believed our message?" (Romans 10:16).

From this follows that only a limited number of people benefit from God's generous offer of forgiveness.

The doctrine, which addresses this reality is:

Limited Atonement

"To atone" from Middle English means "make or become united or reconciled". God puts us from the state of depravity into a position of reunifying us with Himself despite our lack of merit. The Bible, taken in its totality, teaches that God's reconciliation or making peace and unity with us is available to all people but a limited number receive it.

"He is the atoning sacrifice for our sins, and not only for ours but also for the sins of the whole world"
(1John 2:2)

"Who (God|) wants all people to be saved and to come to a knowledge of the truth."
(1 Tim 2:4)

We can see that Jesus provided salvation for all people but not all would respond to His call. God does not want them to die, but He will not force them to live with Him if they really do not want that. Adam and Eve were created righteous and free, and they chose to rebel against God. This does not mean that that was God's will for them. He warned them that they will die and the only way back into relationship with Him was if they truly repent. This is true for all of us. We have a way back and God will enable us to walk it all through but He will not make us do it if we deeply, definitely and truly do not want it.

"Say to them, 'As surely as I live, declares the Sovereign Yahweh, I take no pleasure in the death of the wicked, but rather that they turn from their

ways and live. Turn! Turn from your evil ways! Why will you die, people of Israel?' (Ez 31:11)

One may be "wicked", but God is still good to them and He wants them to turn back i.e. repent and be spared the consequences of their sins.

Not all people who are called heed God's words.

"Isaiah cries out concerning Israel: "Though the number of the Israelites be like the sand by the sea, only the remnant will be saved." Romans 9:27

"But since you refuse to listen when I call and no one pays attention when I stretch out my hand," Proverbs 1:24

God has not stopped calling people and He calls all people to turn to Him yet clearly not all do so. This is not due to lack of desire on the side of God. God is loving and He loves to save all people.

"Because God so loved the world that He gave His only begotten son so that no one who believes in Him perishes but has eternal life" (John 3:16).

We notice here how the salvation is made possible for the world. God's desire is the world to be saved and come to Him, but those who trust in Him and accept Jesus when given this opportunity can receive His salvation.

Sometimes people say: "What if some people never heard of Jesus?". That is a fair question, and we know that God is absolutely just and knows everything. God knows what they would have done had they been exposed to the Gospel of Jesus and if they would have genuinely repented.

Therefore, to recap, we were all in a state of total depravity, going astray from the One who loves us more than anybody, our Maker, our Heavenly Father, but God calls us all to salvation and makes it possible for us to change and be resurrected to a new life for Him. This is unconditional. We do not deserve it, we made our choice, but God chooses not to end it there and instead makes the next step, showing radical love to us. He makes this step before we were even there. Many of us respond to this love, enabled by Him, (we could not do it on our own), and the image of God in each of us is brought back to life as it is meant to be - to glorify God by doing His good works. This spiritual resurrection is limited to those who accept God by repentance and trusting in Jesus. It is impossible without God's intervention though.

This radical intervention is called:

Irresistible Grace

A young (in his thirties) Jewish teacher, called Saul, a member of the ultra- orthodox grouping amongst the elite in the temple city of Jerusalem, the Pharisees, had a very unpleasant, but in his mind, absolutely necessary job to do: he had to protect the faith of his forefathers against an abhorrent Jewish sect, whose adherents called themselves "Christians" and which, like a wildfire, was gaining ever more followers and sympathisers in the spiritual capital of Israel and well beyond. He had a lead about a group of such sectarians residing in Damascus, Syria, about 180 miles (13 days on a donkey) up north from Jerusalem. It was an arduous journey, all those sand winds, raging heatwaves and the tiring unobstructed sun. Naturally, most of his fellows were exhausted and dreamt of a break in their journey, but they pressed on as hard as they could to keep up with Paul, who was showing no sign of fatigue and no desire to rest. His determination was both inspiring, but also so onerous, to the point when they likely entertained the dilemma that maybe he had been given special powers by God to do this important task or alternatively he was a fanatical madman. It was not possible for any natural or human obstacle to overcome Saul's iron will. In the sacks on the donkeys' backs, one could hear the jingling of the metal shackles and instruments of torture which he had prepared for those miscreant Jewish Christians. He had to bring them back to the fold by hook or by crook. Later on he would admit that he aimed to make them, through torture, to blaspheme against their Lord called Jesus. He was possibly reasoning that once they spoke up against their "Saviour" they would not be able to go back to Him and then the only option would be to rejoin their former "mainstream" Jewish religion. Perhaps he was fanatical, which is what they likely suspected about him. Who engages in such twisted actions of physical harm and reverse psychology for the sake of denying somebody the right to worship God as they see fit? This was not the first time he did this and with experience in pursuing and punishing, he was getting good at it and very efficient.

Nothing could stop Saul's drive and his chasing of what he believed to be right. Then something incredible happened. As he neared Damascus on his journey, suddenly a light from heaven flashed around him. He fell to the ground and heard a voice say to him,

"Saul, Saul, why do you persecute me?"

"Who are you, Lord?" Saul asked.

"I am Jesus, whom you are persecuting," he replied.

"Now get up and go into the city, and you will be told what you must do."

The men travelling with Saul stood there speechless; they heard the sound but did not see anyone. Saul got up from the ground, but when he opened his eyes, he could see nothing. So, they led him by the hand into Damascus. For three days he was blind and did not eat or drink anything. (Acts 9:3-9)

Later Saul, who became the apostle Paul, remembered some more words which Jesus told him on the road to Damascus and what it meant to him:

We all fell to the ground, and I heard a voice saying to me in Aramaic, 'Saul, Saul, why do you persecute me? It is hard for you to kick against the prodding stick (Acts 26:14)

But when God, who set me apart from my mother's womb and called me by his grace, was pleased to reveal his Son to me so that I might preach him among the Gentiles, my immediate response was not to consult any human being (Gal 1:15,16).

The grace of our Lord was poured out on me abundantly, along with the faith and love that are in Christ Jesus. ***Here is a trustworthy saying that deserves full acceptance: Christ Jesus came into the world to save sinners—of whom I am the worst. But for that very reason I was shown mercy so that in me, the worst of sinners, Christ Jesus might display his immense patience as an example for those who would believe in him and receive eternal life. Now to the King eternal, immortal, invisible, the only God, be honor and glory for ever and ever.*** Amen. (1 Tim 1: 14-17)

Notice how Saul had been determined to live in his own way, believing that this was the right way to be. If anybody had goals in life that was him. Jesus though told him that it was hard 'to kick against the prodding stick'. This was a tool which farmers used to guide their livestock in the right direction. Saul did not know that he had been chosen to belong to Christ, and that the course of his life would have to do a180-degree turn. From a total disbeliever in Jesus and persecutor of His church, Saul/Paul became a teacher and apostle of God's words, wrote about 40% of the New Testament and gave his life for Christ, both serving the church and physically. Something happened which he could not resist. He met the author of his destiny. Of course, he had freedom to reject what God had asked him to be and do, but he was 'elected', based on God's foreknowledge even before he was born, like all of us who have decided to follow Jesus, to turn to the Saviour away from their sins, to be saved and to do God's will. To some people the grace of God is "resistible". They are offered salvation, but they refuse it. It might be the case that they are not elected to receive God's forgiveness, not because God does not want this for them, but because they choose to resist His will. Some people resist for a time and then give themselves up to God. This means that they were known by God before they were born and they were elected for this. Others never give themselves to God which goes to show that that is their existential, eternal choice to be separate from God. In the case with the religious teachers, the Pharisees, we are told that God's will was for them to be saved, but they refused to obey and act accordingly. When God calls somebody, they had better act and not delay.

All the people, even the tax collectors, when they heard Jesus' words, acknowledged that God's way was right, because they had been baptized by John. But the Pharisees and the experts in the law rejected God's purpose for themselves because they had not been baptized by John. (Luke 7:29,30).

As God's co-workers we urge you not to receive God's grace in vain (2 Cor 6:1).

Paul said that

"the grace of our Lord was poured on me abundantly"
(1 Tim 1:14a),

but also urged the Christians to "not receive God's grace in vain" and

"But by the grace of God I am what I am, and his grace to me was not in vain. No, I worked harder than all of them--yet not I, but the grace of God that was with me." (1Cor 15:10)

We see how the apostle Paul, indeed like all of us, was a slave of a depraved sinful nature, and it would take God's grace, His undeserved benevolence, despite the very well-deserved punishment for his sins, to turn him around. This happened and will happen to all who have been chosen for salvation - they will respond to God's grace and it will not be in vain. For them the grace of God is simply irresistible. They will answer the call and come to their Heavenly Father. There will be others who are offered the same grace, but it will not benefit them because they did not accept God's gift of their spiritual regeneration. We conclude that without God's grace we cannot come to Him. It is His work that makes this possible and our response, made possible by Him, takes possession of the benefits of His work.

God's grace continues to work throughout the course of the life of the believer and ensures that they are supported, consistently, in order that they can cross the finishing line of their mortal lives victoriously and be with God forever more.

This work of God in us and its end effect is called:

Perseverance of the Saints

We, without God, are slaves of our deprived, sinful (in its tendency) nature, and it takes God's intervention of grace and regeneration through His Spirit and Word for us to turn to Him and be saved. Some people, as we said, can resist the grace of God. God enables your choice but will not force it unless He knows that it is your free will to accept His ways. Once people receive Jesus, they do not stop being attacked by sin and deception from the enemy, and their sinful nature may falter at times. This is the case because of the free choice available. God values our freedom. Being saved now does not mean that this is forever:

"We have come to share in Christ, if indeed we hold our original conviction firmly to the very end. (Hebrews 3:14)"

It becomes a permanent reality if we "hold our original conviction" meaning that we keep on choosing to obey and follow Jesus. Then one may reasonably ask: "What if I stop following Him? I am just a weak human being." The answer is that if we are on our own, surely, we will stop following God. We would be soon tricked and lured into self-defeat. The enemy, 'the father of lies', is stronger than us if we depend on our own choices. The same way in which we depended entirely on God to come to us and resurrect us from our deathly slumber of ignorance and a tendency to sin, when we were without Him, we now also constantly depend on Him. We cannot do anything without Him. And we have the assurance from God that He will not leave us nor forsake us:

"Be strong and courageous. Do not be afraid or terrified because of them, for the Lord your God goes with you; he will never leave you nor forsake you."
(Deuteronomy 31:6)."

"I will not leave you as orphans; I will come to you"
(John 14:18).

"I am with you always, even unto the end of the world." Amen."
(Matthew 28:20b)

Jesus through the Holy Spirit is constantly taking care of each believer. His unceasing involvement with us guarantees that we will be preserved and enter the Kingdom of God when the time arrives. In the meantime, we grow daily through the work of God's word and Spirit in us and we become ever more like Jesus, which means we acquire His mind (repentance) and do His works.

To be saved is not a one-off solution. It is a daily walk and growth in the grace and guidance of God.

I will outline three broad stages of repentance and how it bears on our salvation from the sins and their consequences, but now is the moment to burden you a little bit with some Biblical Hebrew and Biblical Greek and explain the meaning of the word for "repentance" in both languages. I will not actually be a burden, you will likely enjoy it, just bear with me!

The Hebrew word "to repent" is *shoob* and it literally means to return. For example, in **Genesis 8:9** we read about the bird which Noah sent from his ship to seek dry land:

But the dove found no place to rest its foot, and it returned (Shoob) to him into the ship.

The word shows that one is going on their way, away from a place or somebody, but they decide to turn around at 180 degrees and go back, "return", to where they came from.

In **Malachi 3:7** God says:

***"From the days of your fathers you have turned aside from my commandments and have not kept them. Return* (shoob) *to Me and I will return* (shoob) *to you" says Yahweh of the Hosts. But you say, "How shall we return* (shoob)?"**

Here the people of God, Israel, we are told, have "turned aside" and God asks them to repent or return to Him and keep His words. They had to come back to where they left from - God.

This state of "being astray" is something which is the case with all people before they come to God for forgiveness. There is no person who has never been astray in some way from God's good and right words.

The prophet Isaiah says:

We all, like sheep, have gone astray, each of us has turned to our own way;
(Isaiah 53:6a).

This includes all people. None of us can say that we never or will never be able to fall astray from God's way. God tells us to return, to repent, change our ways and align them with His.

The Hebrew word for repentance indicates an outward change of behaviour, which is expressed in returning to God. For this to happen though one needs to experience change of mind. First you decide, and then you do.

The Greek word describes this psychological and spiritual state of mind behind the appropriate works of repentance. When in Mark chapter 1, Jesus said "Repent", He used a word which comes from the Greek word *Metanoia*. The prefix *Meta* signifies something “beyond” or “behind” which determines or holds the outside appearance. Your mind thinks in a certain way before you behave in according to that thought. The word *Metanoia* is translated in English as “repentance” or “conversion” and it denotes transformation of one’s heart or mind and behaviours, in accordance with God. From Greek it literally means “change of mind or thinking”.

We see that our behaviour is a product of our mind which, as we already pointed out, reflects our spiritual nature, our deep spiritual attitude toward God.

I cannot overemphasise that the only way out of the wrong way of thinking, and the change of behaving contrary to God is possible, in its fullness, when God touches our hearts. Before He regenerates or restores us, we are dead in our sins and toward Him.

We observe three broad types of practical repentance. One is when somebody is drawn to God, comes to Him in some way but never surrenders to Him. The second type is when one comes to God and surrenders to Him for good. The third type of repentance is after we have surrendered to God but fall in some sin. I will discuss these three next because the distinctions between them are important.

COMING TO GOD, BUT NOT REALLY

A wild and weird man, whom we mentioned above, 2000 years ago appeared in the wilderness and began to scream out:

"Repent, the Lord is coming! Make your ways right before the Lord"
(Mk 1:3).

This was John the Baptist. He was baptising all who were willing to repent. Many people were coming to him and getting baptised, but he said to the crowds coming for baptism:

You brood of vipers! Who warned you to flee from the coming wrath?
(Luke 3:7)

He noticed that some people got baptised for the wrong reasons. Some came because it had become fashionable. Others felt that something was wrong in their lives and they wanted to make it right. Some others were simply afraid of what this prophet of God was saying:

"The axe is already at the root of the trees, and every tree that does not produce good fruit will be cut down and thrown into the fire."(Luke 3:9).

Hence, they ran to John to get this ritual done.

As we read the story of John, we learn that he said that the people needed true repentance for which the evidence was "good fruit" which meant a changed lifestyle. People asked how their life should change and so he advised them.

"What should we do then?" the crowd asked.

John answered,

"Anyone who has two shirts should share with the one who has none, and anyone who has food should do the same."

Even tax collectors came to be baptized. "Teacher," they asked, "what should we do?"

"Don't collect any more than you are required to," he told them.

Then some soldiers asked him, "And what should we do?"

He replied,

"Don't extort money and don't accuse people falsely—be content with your pay." (Luke 3:10-14)

They had to begin to care for those who have less. They should not abuse anybody. They should not talk lies about anybody. These are some of the pieces of advice he gave them. He also said:

"I baptize you with water. But one who is more powerful than I will come, the straps of whose sandals I am not worthy to untie. He will baptize you with the Holy Spirit and fire.
(Luke 3:16b)

He was urging them to be ready for Jesus and receive Him. The fact that some were baptised did not mean that they had really repented and decided to change for good. It did not mean that they were really committed to obedience toward God. John's severe warning was for them. They may be baptised but they are not yet saved. They needed to repent and receive Jesus as their Messiah and Lord. We see people, perhaps some of us are exactly like this, who come to God but are not serious. They want even to be baptised but have no intention to surrender to Him. This is a quasi-repentance - apparent, but not real. It has some appearance of turning to God but is not an actual decision to come to Him and be His follower. Such a type of "repentance" cannot save anyone. It may lull one's conscience into a slumber that something good and beneficial happened, leading to salvation, but unless the baptism or prayer for receiving Jesus was sincere and one really wants to change their life and commit to this by surrendering to Christ, they have not yet been born again and been saved. Repentance is a real turning, a conversion and a change of mind toward obedience to Jesus.

TRULY REPENTING

In Jesus' time, when He was amongst the people in human form, He had many sympathisers, who were not disciples. Many marvelled at His miracles and believed in Him, but they would not openly surrender to Him and follow His teaching and learn from Him.

John, one of Jesus' apostles, relates:

Yet at the same time many even among the leaders believed in him. But because of the Pharisees they would not openly acknowledge their faith for fear they would be put out of the synagogue; for they loved human praise more than praise from God. (John 12:42,43)

To "acknowledge" their faith meant to start living out as Jesus says. This included openly challenging injustice. They could not bear this. They loved the approval of the sinful world so they would never confront its bad works. This did not please God.

One of those people, who was a part of the 70-member strong Jewish ruling body based around the temple in Jerusalem, was Nicodemus.

He came to Jesus at night and said,

"Rabbi, we know that you are a teacher who has come from God. For no one could perform the signs you are doing if God were not with him."

Jesus replied,

"Very truly I tell you, no one can see the kingdom of God unless they are born again. (John 3:2,3)

Jesus was very direct; He did not try to placate and make Nicodemus feel great and save him the truth. It was a matter of life and death. That is why Jesus told him that he needed to be born again, come to God for real not just cheer from the side and keep on living for the approval of others. God must be first place. Quasi-repentance will not help Nicodemus if it does not progress into a true repentance. Unless this transition were made Nicodemus simply and clearly could not "see/enter the Kingdom of God".

Nicodemus was startled. He would go on to say that he does not even know the meaning of being born again is. He wondered if it is possible. Is it a physical rebirth?

How can someone be born when they are old?" Nicodemus asked.

"Surely they cannot enter a second time into their mother's womb to be born!" (John 3:4)

Nicodemus did not understand that God was working in his heart, but he needed to give himself to the Spirit of God and to follow through with that commitment. It was his decision to make.

Jesus said,

"Very truly I tell you, no one can enter the kingdom of God unless they are born of water and the Spirit "
(John 3:5).

The water was a symbol of repentance, a changing of one's mind and a decision to turn around for good, when sins are washed away and the new person in the image and glory of God raises up. When a person does this, led by the Spirit, because they want to follow God, and not due to public or private pressures and because they are trying to conform, then they are really "born again" and can see and enter the Kingdom of God.

"How can this be?"
Nicodemus asked (John 3:9).

Nicodemus could not understand that being with God is not a halfhearted affair. He had to go all in. He wanted to continue doing what he thought was right, without allowing himself to be informed and transformed by God's words, and in some way respect Jesus, without obedience, and hopefully enter the Kingdom of God and be saved.

Jesus diagnosed his problem very precisely:

Very truly I tell you, we speak of what we know, and we testify to what we have seen, but still, you

people do not accept our testimony. I have spoken to you of earthly things and you do not believe; how then will you believe if I speak of heavenly things? No one has ever gone into heaven except the one who came from heaven—the Son of Man. Just as Moses lifted up the snake in the wilderness, so the Son of Man must be lifted up, that everyone who believes may have eternal life in him (John 3:11-15)

Nicodemus and his colleagues did not accept what Jesus was saying. They would not accept even the basics, let alone if He went deeper into heavenly things. That is why they were not born again, and this included Nicodemus. He had to realise that Jesus was the only One who came from heaven and only by believing in Him, which would lead to learning from Him and obeying Him, could he have eternal life.

Nicodemus needed to accept all that Jesus and His apostles said about Him, who He was: the Saviour, Lord and God and accept His words of instruction for thinking and living. There was and there is no other way.

This is the true repentance when we surrender to God in this way, putting our trust in Jesus and eagerly learning and following His words.

A person does not get perfect in their thinking and behaviour right away, but if they look with trust to Jesus and decide, sincerely and seriously, to follow Him means that from that moment onward they receive eternal life and become part of God's family.

One may ask: "Should I not become sinless first and then be accepted by God?". Notice the promise of Jesus:

Just as Moses lifted up the snake in the wilderness, so the Son of Man must be lifted up, that everyone who believes may have eternal life in him (John 14,15)

"The snake" which Moses lifted in the wilderness was made from copper or bronze and it was necessary because the Israelites had sinned against God. When His protection was withdrawn due to their sin of grumbling and talking badly about God, they were attacked by poisonous snakes. Some died but others asked Moses for help and God told him to make a copper serpent and hang it on a piece of wood and everyone who looked at it would receive the ability in their body to neutralise the poison of the reptile. They had simply to look and do nothing. Afterwards they were expected to be obedient, but they had to remain alive first to change their attitude and lifestyle. That is how we come to Jesus and put our trust in Him and His work for us on the wood - the Cross - and we are 'quickened' (made alive) by God through faith. Then we are no more dead in our sins and we become able to learn and be like Jesus. We cannot become sinless on our own no more than the Israelites could remain alive after the biting of the snakes. You and I need to receive and trust in Jesus which produces life in us and then we will be counted as if sinless, as though the poison of sin never affected us, and on the path to practical sinlessness which will increasingly progress in our lives. Nobody whilst on earth, in flesh, is sinless at all time but God makes us able to live a life in which we do not make practice of sin. It does not mean we will never sin after we received Jesus, but it means we cannot live and have a lifestyle of sin. Sin is not a permanent feature in our life although it may and indeed occurs, not as a complicit practice and lifestyle, in the lives of all Christians. If we do not make practice of sin and choose to live without challenging it, we are born again. and we have eternal life. God is teaching how to live a blessed and happy life of holiness and bliss in His ways. Here we come to the last part of the repentance process which is:

REPENTANCE AS A LIFESTYLE

You have truly repented and put your trust in Jesus. You mean business. You want to follow God wherever He leads you and obey Him. You are born again. You are part of God's family. Nothing can part you from His hand.

You are still on earth though and the devil and his system, the sinful world, is still there trying to pull you back into the state of being dead in sin.

Jesus says that:

"Temptations to sin are sure to come"
(Luke 17:1)

He said to the apostle Peter:

"Simon, Simon! Indeed, Satan has asked for you, that he may sift you as wheat. But I have prayed for you, that your faith should not fail; and when you have returned to Me, strengthen your brethren."

But he said to Him,

"Lord, I am ready to go with You, both to prison and to death."

Then He said,

"I tell you, Peter, the rooster shall not crow this day before you will deny three times that you know Me." (Luke 22:31-34)

Peter was born again, and he was a sincere believer. Jesus told Him that his name and those of the other apostles, except for Judas Iscariot, are written in the Book of Life in heaven:

"...rejoice that your names are written in heaven." (Luke 10:20b)

Yet, Jesus told Peter that he would fall into terrible sin - to deny Jesus before people. This automatically meant that he would be denied before God.

"Whoever denies me before others, I also will deny before my Father who is in heaven" (Matthew 10:33)

Also, Jesus told him that Peter "will turn back" meaning that he would not remain in sin. Not only will he turn back but he will serve to build up his brothers and sisters in their faith. It is desirable to be able to say that once you are baptised and accept Jesus and follow Him you will never sin. This is not the Biblical picture though. The Bible is clear that one may fall into sin and it urges us to be gentle with such a person and encourage them to come back to God.

My friends, if anyone is caught in any transgression, you who are spiritual should

restore such a one in a spirit of gentleness. Keep watch on yourself, lest you too be tempted (Gal 6:1).

It is one thing to fall into sin but another to make it your lifestyle. The gentleness in this approach to restoration from sin is aimed at making the person not to make a practice of bad behaviour and remain in sin. Remaining in sin will mean that you receive judgement and will not be with God. But God is gentle, and He has provided a way of salvation from the sins. He forgives you and changes you, so you would not make a practice of sin.

How does He do that? It is as with our salvation - it is His work which encourages and elicits our cooperation.

There are several parts of this dealing with sin and ensuring a life of changed mind and behaviour, a life of repentance.

Before we investigate them let us point out that Jesus expects from us to lead a life of constant repentance.

"Be like those who are waiting for their master to come home from the wedding feast, so that they may open the door to him at once when he comes and knocks". (Luke 12:36)

This means to be constantly ready for Jesus to come. If repentance is an unwavering condition for salvation and for entry into the Kingdom of God, then we must be repentant as a matter of lifestyle.

We must be aware if we have sinned and repent from it and never allow it to fester and keep on growing because:

sin, when it is full-grown, gives birth to death. (James 1:15b).

Not every sin will kill one right away spiritually like denying Jesus, but every sin when fully developed kills. There are two ways to be aware that you have sinned and need repentance before it takes away your life and position as God's child and saint: through your conscience and through God's Word.

The Holy Spirit uses your conscience and ensures that He reminds you what you have done, not to make you feel in despair, but to come to Jesus for forgiveness and cleansing. When your conscience is alive, then it is a great tool in the work of the Holy Spirit to keep you holy. It though cannot be kept properly alive for long if it is not based on the Word of God, the Bible. If the Bible, as taught by Jesus and His apostles, is not constantly permeating into our conscience, we will not be able to make a difference between what is good before God and what is bad. This state of moral confusion is characteristic for those who do not have the foundation of God's words.

Prophet Isaiah warns against this state of confusion:

Woe to those who call evil good and good evil, who put darkness for light and light for darkness, who put bitter for sweet and sweet for bitter. (Isaiah 5:20)

When people depart from God's counsel then morality becomes relative. Some things may be good for you but not good for me and vice versa. Rather the most important thing is that what we consider good is good before God and what we consider bad is bad before God. For this we need the light of the Bible shining into our human, fallen, nature's shadow.

In Proverbs 28:9 we read:

If anyone turns a deaf ear to my instruction, even their prayers are detestable.

When someone does not want to listen to what God says they may put themselves in the position that they pray with "detestable" prayers. "Detestable prayers" are those going against what is good in the sight of God.

The Bible is the guide and instruction on how to live a life with a changed mind. God encouraged Joshua, the Israelites' leader:

"This Book of the Law shall not depart from your mouth, but you shall meditate on it day and night, so that you may be careful to do according to all that is written in it. For then you will make your way prosperous, and then you will have good success" (Joshua 1:8).

He had to make sure, more important than anything else, that the Book of the Law, the Book from God, "does not depart from his eyes" but he reads it, thinks about it deeply, constantly, by measuring everything in his life against its standard, speaks it and does it. Therefore, the first ingredient of the lifestyle of repentance is to **ensure you study the Bible regularly and use it**.

Unless you base your life on the Word of God you are a nonstarter.

When you read the Bible, it reveals things about you which need correction. If it reveals a sin and something which you must change then, once you realise that you have sinned, **regret it.**

Regretting is the opposite of rebellion. When you regret in a good way you do not look to excuse yourself and make it out to be as if it is nothing to do with you. Circumstances and people might have led you to make the wrong decisions you made, but you were still the person making those decisions. Take responsibility. Do not hide behind someone else. Do not ignore that there are often mitigating circumstances but these do not take away the wrong. Regret is not a word which is liked by many people these days. It is surely an unpleasant feeling, but the Bible presents one type of regret which is good. It is a form of grief which arises not out of desperation that things cannot change, but it is deeply hopeful that God investigates your heart and gives you a change of mind - repentance, which leads to salvation, in other words good things.

For godly grief produces a repentance that leads to salvation without regret, whereas worldly grief produces death.
(2 Cor 7:10)

This form of regret or grief attaches bad experience in your mind with the wrong thing you have done. This changes your mind so that you do not like this thing but rather you hate it and are repulsed by it. This is a good thing. Once it does its work you will have no regrets afterwards because you have learnt a valuable lesson by taking the wrongdoing seriously to the point of regret and you know that God has carried out important work inside of you for your own good. Such regret is based on you caring to please God. It occurs because God is more important for you than anything and anybody. The results are a blessing and joy.

Once you regret genuinely the bad thing you have done, said, or thought, you make sure that you say that regret. This is a **confession**. You can share with people, if they are good confidants, or if you hurt someone you have to acknowledge this and apologise to them, but you confess primarily before God. He is the One against whom every sin is committed, and He is the One who can forgive and make you a new person. King David committed grievous offences. Tradition believes him to have written the Psalms. We read in Psalm 51:

Against you, you only, have I sinned and done what is evil in your sight; so, you are right in your verdict and justified when you judge.

Ultimately, when we do something bad it is against God and who He is. We should bear this in mind. We should also remember that God remains our Father, even when we are wrong. He is not an enemy who is mad at us. He hates sin because it is bad for us and others, it runs against who He is, the loving Father, who cares for us and is for us.

If someone thinks about God as vindictive and judgmental, they do not know God because

God is love (1 John 4:8).

He loves to forgive. Notice this:

You, Lord, are forgiving and good, abounding in love to all who call to you.* *(Psalm 86:5)

Your act of confession before God is “calling to Him” and it leads to abundant love from Him to you. We need to be honest about it. God forgives, but we should realise that wrong is wrong and admit it. This cleanses our conscience and opens the door to perfecting our character. We do not wish to cover up what is not good. The Psalmist says:

Then I acknowledged my sin to you and did not cover up my iniquity. I said, "I will confess my transgressions to Yahweh." And you forgave the guilt of my sin.* *(Psalm 32:5).

Confession brings forgiveness. The Apostle John reminds us:

If we confess our sins, he is faithful and just and will forgive us our sins and purify us from all unrighteousness.* *(1 John 1:9)

It sounds too easy, too good to be true, but it is based on the most precious sacrifice and payment ever given for the sins of the world - Jesus Christ on the cross. For this to work one needs to

Trust in Jesus Christ as their Saviour.

We said that God can forgive all sins because ultimately, they are done against Him as Creator and against His creation. God loves to forgive, but that does not come easy because God, who is loving, is also just and holy. This created a serious problem for us which only God can solve. If He lets people go without a just retribution for their sins, then that shows that He does not care for justice. If a judge lets a criminal go just like that or because of other good works they did separately from the crime, they are not a just judge. Every crime should receive its punishment. The justice of God, which is part of His character, demands that this happens. This is who He is, and He cannot change. This means that all people should receive the just consequences for their sins. This includes the sin of rejecting their Creator, which is the fundamental sin, leading to all others. God can mete out judgment and He assures us that this would happen in this life and in the next one. If someone got away with crime and sin in this life, they will surely be judged eternally:

God "will repay each person according to what they have done.
(Rom 2:6)

The ultimate judgement is eternal separation from Him. God does not force anybody to be with Him. Sinning without repentance shows that one does not want to be with God.

God though does not want to punish people, let alone have them eternally separated from Himself. We already said that He is loving. All good things come from Him ultimately. The Epistle of James tells us:

Every good and perfect gift is from above, coming down from the Father of the heavenly lights, who does not change like shifting shadows
(James 1:17)

How can God show that justice must be done and at the same time does not judge the sinners (all of us) because He loves them?

Consequently, when Christ came into the world, he said,

"Sacrifices and offerings you have not desired, but a body have you prepared for me" (Hebrews 10:5).

In the Old Testament, where God instructed the Israelites to offer various sacrifices, they were central to the worship of the people. They were a reminder that sin is bad and not easily dismissed, but it costs lives. About 30% of the Law of Moses deals with sacrifices. Forgiveness was only possibly if you obeyed the instruction in the Law and through a sacrifice admitted that one had been wrong, evil was bad and cost a great deal. After this repentance and sacrifice for sins, God demonstrated His goodness and mercy.

Jesus says in the above verse from Hebrews that now it is not going to be animal sacrifice but instead His own body, which will take away fully the sins of all, who come to trust in Him. God does not now want the sacrifice of animals, but He wants to take away our sins personally and He does that through His Son, Jesus Christ, who is God in human form.

Jesus says again:

I am the living bread that came down from heaven. Whoever eats this bread will live forever. This bread is my flesh, which I will give for the life of the world." (John 6:51).

Some of the sacrifices in the temple were eaten and some burnt. Burning corresponded to the eating by God. The eating and burning of sacrifices symbolised how God and humankind had met in the sacrifice and God's justice was satisfied and His love poured over the person. The sacrifice of Jesus was where this literally happened - God and humanity became integrated and one in a sense that through accepting Jesus, we became part of the divine nature by receiving pardon for his sins and being adopted by God.

Thus, He has given us through these things [His own glory and goodness] His precious and very great promises, so that through them you may become partakers of the divine nature, having escaped from the corruption that is in the world because of sinful desire.
(2 Peter 1:4)

In Christ God shows to us His glory and goodness, by not only sparing us from our sins and their full consequences, but by making us have His great promises which we adopt through faith, one of which is to direct us away from sinful desires. We join His nature and start liking what He likes and dislike what He dislikes. That is why the sacrifice of Jesus is so important. It provides the means where we imperfect people meet the perfect God and join in one spirit with Him. When we ask for forgiveness, this is the only ground on which we can receive God's pardon, that we already, through Jesus, have a special relationship with Him. If we do not wish to join God at this level which He has provided through the sacrifice of His Son, then we must be perfect to come close to the perfect God. Nobody however is holy and perfect. God tells us that nobody can see His face and remain alive:

But," he said,

"you cannot see my face, for no one may see me and live." (Exodus 33:20)

God said this to Moses. Most people are not at Moses' level, but rather much lower. It is not possible to claim that one does not need the sacrifice of Jesus to be holy and perfect. To say however that nobody can come close to God whatever is to doubt God's desire to be close to us and to be our Father. The only place where we meet God, closely and intimately, is in Jesus and this is provided by God because He loves us.

Through Jesus, by trust in Him, we have access to the holy God, who now is our Father.

Let us then with confidence draw near to the throne of grace, that we may receive mercy and find grace to help in time of need. (Hebrews 4:16)

This encouragement is valid for all needs and all times but particularly so at those times when we are dealing with sin. If you are in sin now, the best thing to do is come sincerely to your Father, trusting in Jesus.

My little children, I am writing these things to you so that you may not sin. But if anyone does sin, we have an advocate with the Father, Jesus Christ the righteous. (1 John 2:1)

We are guided and helped not to sin, but in time of need and sin we have Jesus. Nobody can help us, but Jesus. We must trust in His advocacy for us. He is the righteous One who takes away the sins of the unrighteous and justifies them through His work for them.

You know that he appeared to take away sins, and in him there is no sin. (1 John 3:5)

When we trust entirely on Jesus, not on our own works and merit, let alone someone else, we receive His full support and through Him full exoneration and God's blessing, which He loves to bestow on us.

Therefore, since we have been justified through faith, we have peace with God through our Lord Jesus Christ (Romans 5:1)

God and you have a relationship of peace and what a peace it is! He is now your Heavenly Father!

When we think about these things, we feel joy. It is natural if you have realised your sins through reading God's Word, regretted them because they steal from you and run against God, admitted, and confessed them with faith in Jesus and trust in His perfect love for you which he demonstrated in His sacrifice and constant advocacy for you. It is natural then to receive the joy of God in you. How can you be not happy about all that God did for you? He pardoned you and adopted you! This is the best thing that you can get, and it is because of His grace it is yours as a gift. If you do not feel joy in your heart and gratitude you must go through the above steps and slowly think about these things and God would give you understanding about what you have in Christ. But if you received the joy of God and you feel this joy and gratitude, then you can burst into praise and thanksgiving! Regret attaches negative feelings to sin, but joy expressed in gratitude imprints on you the positive attitude toward your Father, which should never leave you because this gift is meant to stay with you forever. You have constant access to God. You are family. Joy, based on what God did for you, affirms your faith and rejects any attempt of the devil to make you feel bad about yourself, unworthy and keep distant from God. You are worthy because of Jesus!

Nehemiah said,

"Go and enjoy choice food and sweet drinks, and send some to those who have nothing prepared. This day is holy to our Lord. Do not grieve, for the joy of Yahweh is your strength." (Nehemiah 8:10)

Maybe that is good advice: go and give someone lunch and tell them what Jesus did for you, how He saved you from your sins and about the repentance He gave you. The bottom line is to be happy for what God did for you. This is a holy experience when you experience God's grace and love and full forgiveness.

Before you go there is one more thing. You must **decide to learn from Jesus and change to be like Him.**

Full repentance means that you decide that you will live differently. God will enable you to live a life of righteousness and integrity. You may slide here or there but remember He is always with you. You must devise a strategy for how you will learn from God and shun evils. It revolves around the Word of God, the Bible. Ensure you read it regularly and thoughtfully. Think over it. Get to be part of a church where they explain the Bible and you will find new friends who are also committed to live life good before God. “Show me your friends and I will show you your future”. There is some truth in this. Hang around with people who are on the same journey as you. God will make you grow. You will progress and become ever more like Jesus. You will not be able to live in sin because the kernel of God will be in you and you keep maintaining it. You have been given a new nature of righteousness and God is in you.

Those who have been born of God refuse to practice sin, because God’s seed abides in them; they cannot go on sinning, because they have been born of God (1 John 3:9).

That is your real you. The true you created in the Image of God. The closer you walk with Him the more like Him you will be.

Keep up with God’s Word and renew your mind through it. This will make you do great works for God.

Do not conform to the pattern of this world but be transformed by the renewing of your mind. Then you will be able to test and approve what God's will is--his good, pleasing, and perfect will (Romans 12:2)

By doing this you will do good things, things pleasing to God, perfect things in accordance with His will. Your life can unfold to its true God given potential. You will be satisfied as never you have been before because you have found your home. You are not just a function of your genetic makeup, environment, and life experiences but you have “the seed” of

God in you. You are spiritual. The Spirit of God is in you and will continue to abide in you.

Lastly, we need to answer this question: “what if I sin again?”

We are called to live a life where our conscience does not judge us.

For I am conscious of nothing against myself (1 Cor 4:4a).

Our normal state of being should be that we are conscious of nothing against us, whilst we have regular time of reading, listening and meditation on God’s Word. This results in powerful prayers:

Beloved, if our heart does not condemn us, we have confidence before God; and receive from him anything we ask, because we keep his commands and do what pleases him. (1 John 3:21,22).

If you have a pure conscience whilst sincerely learning and studying the Bible, then whatever you ask will be done to you.

But if you sin then **without delay** you should go back to God and follow the steps above: regret, confess, trust in Jesus alone, be happy that He is faithful to remove your sin and make the decision to continue your walk with Christ.

Even stubborn, addictive sins like alcoholism, drugs, porn, gambling etc. get their hold on you broken, when you fully follow the steps outlined with sincerity and seriousness. It helps when without waiting you repent immediately.

If we confess our sins, he is faithful and just and will forgive us our sins and purify us from all unrighteousness (John 1:9).

He is truly faithful and just. God's love is not a fleeting one. He can justly forgive you because Jesus paid for your sins. On the cross Jesus literally took our sins and literally He is freeing us from them.

Only **repent and trust in Him** –

...Jesus Christ the faithful witness, the firstborn of the dead, and the ruler of kings on earth. To him who loves us and has freed us from our sins by his blood and has made us to be a kingdom and priests to serve his God and Father— to him be glory and power for ever and ever! Amen.

(*Revelation* 1:5,6)

If you have never come to Jesus with repentance and faith you can do so now by saying these simple but important words:

"God I am not worthy and good as you want me to be, but Jesus came to show me how I should live, died for my sins, overcome the power of death and lives forever to be my advocate and support. I come to you God in Jesus' Name and accept forgiveness of all my sins through Him. Please, lead me and teach me so I can live as your son or daughter. In Christ I pray, amen!"

ABOUT THE AUTHOR

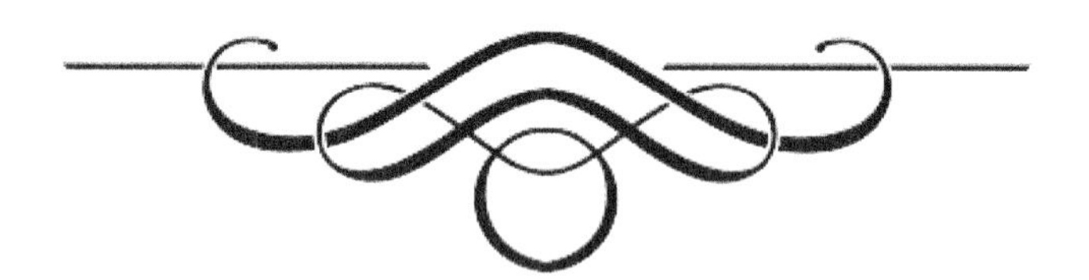

MG Bennett is an ordained Church of England minister and theologian. He holds qualifications in theology (BA, BETI) and English Literature (HECert, University of Cambridge).

Printed in Great Britain
by Amazon